UNCLE JOHN'S
WILD
&
WOOLLY

BATHROOM READER®
FOR KIDS ONLY

by the
Bathroom Readers'
Institute

Bathroom Readers' Press
Ashland, Oregon

UNCLE JOHN'S
WILD AND WOOLLY
BATHROOM READER®
FOR KIDS ONLY

For information, write:
Bathroom Readers' Institute
P.O. Box 1117, Ashland, OR 97520
www.bathroomreader.com

Cover design by Michael Brunsfeld
(brunsfeldo@comcast.com)

Illustrations by John Gaffey

*Uncle John's Wild and Woolly
Bathroom Reader For Kids Only*
by the Bathroom Readers' Institute

ISBN-10: 1-59223-384-8
ISBN-13: 978-1-59223-384-7
Library of Congress Control Number: 2005929787

Printed in the United States of America
First printing 2005
05 06 07 08 09   5 4 3 2 1

READERS' RAVES

Here's what our fans have to say about
Uncle John's Bathroom Reader.

"Your books have everything: facts, humor, silly stuff, and even things that make you go 'hmmm.' I've told my family that the only thing I want for Christmas is another *Bathroom Reader!*"
—**Pat N., age 9**

"I recently led my middle school team to second place in the 'Optimist Brain Bowl.' After every match, judges, teachers, and parents of the opposing team would come up to me, wondering how I knew so much. I simply smiled and said, 'I'd like to thank Uncle John and the entire BRI staff.'"
—**Jamie F., age 13**

"Dear BRI, I really don't like to read. But I really love reading *Bathroom Readers*. Kinda weird, huh?"
—**Joshua B., age 10**

"I'm a fifth grade teacher and I love your books. Tidbits of interesting information are just the things I like to share with my students! I may have to get your book just for kids...they'll devour it!"
—**Kevin W.**

"YOUR BOOKS ROCK!!!!"
—**Chris T., age 15**

TABLE OF CONTENTS

DID YOU KNOW?

• There are approximately 400 million dogs in the world. That's more than all the people in the United States and Canada combined.

• A full-grown white rhino weighs about 5,000 pounds—more than you and all the kids in your class (plus your teacher) put together.

Intro-DOG-tion

Hiya Kids!
Porter the Wonder Dog here.
Because this is a book about animals,
Uncle John asked me—his faithful
pal—to write this introduction. What
an honor! It's almost as fun as chasing
my own tail! (But not quite.)

Well, speaking for animals everywhere, I think you're going to love
this book. Why? Because it's about
ANIMALS! Mammals, mostly: rats, bats, cats, dogs
(woo hoo!), horses, apes, bears, zebras, and some you've
never heard of. Like the meerkat. Know what that is?
(*Hint:* It's not a cat.)

Uncle John also asked me to thank some of the nice
human animals who helped out: Jahnna, Malcolm, and
Maggie did the writing and research (and gave me
treats). John drew the pictures (and gave me treats).
Brian helped find the photographs (and gave me
treats). And Jeff helped Uncle John put it all together
into a book (no treats from Jeff…grrrrr!). As for me, I
was very cute and loving and kept my human friends
happy so they could bring you this great book!

So, on behalf of the entire BRI staff, Happy Reading.

And as Uncle John always says,
Go with the Flow!

THANK YOU!

*The Bathroom Readers' Institute thanks those
people whose help has made this book possible.*

Gordon Javna

Jahnna Beecham

Malcolm Hilgartner

John Gaffey

Jeff Altemus

Brian Boone

Jay Newman

Maggie McLaughlin

Thom Little

Allen Orso

Julia Papps

Jennifer Thornton

John Dollison

Dan Schmitz

Judy Hadlock

Jennifer Browning

Connie Vazquez

Chris Breault

Terri Dunkley

Steven Style Group

Michael Brunsfeld

Christine DeGueron

Sydney Stanley

JoAnn Padgett

Dash and Skye

Maggie Javna

Caitlin and McKenzie

Scarab Media

Laurel, Mana, Dylan,
Barbi, and Chandra

Matthew Furber

Shoba Grace

Annie McIntyre

Gideon and Sam

Porter the Wonder Dog

Thomas Crapper

...and the BRI pets: Bailey, Joe, Napalm,
Gus, Phoenix, Zappa, Sampson, Delilah, Jake,
Blanche, Bella, Henry, Piper Jones, Mystic,
Montana, Glory, & Huckleberry

CAN YOU HEAR ME NOW?

Meet Jack the basset hound from Fulda, Germany. He's got the longest dog ears in the world. And it's official: *Guinness World Records* measured them at 33.2 centimeters each—over a foot long! According to his owners, Claudia and Carsten Baus, Jack's ears flop into his food and water bowls. In fact, they're so long that this lovable one-year-old has a hard time keeping them off the ground and often trips over them when he walks.

RAT FACTS

A rat can fall from a five-story building without getting hurt.

A rat can survive without water longer than a camel.

A group of rats is called a *mischief*.

Rats care for the injured and sick in their group.

Rats can't vomit.

Rats sweat through the bottom of their feet.

A rat can tread water for three days.

Male rats are called *bucks*, females are called *does*, and babies are called *kittens*.

A rat's fur smells like grape soda.

Rats pee as many as 80 times a day.

A rat can produce more than 25,000 droppings in a year.

A rat will grind its teeth when it's happy.

Rats can dive 100 feet underwater.

Rats' teeth grow five inches a year. They gnaw constantly to wear them down.

ZOMBIE DOG

This tale shows you can't keep a good dog down.

Sweetie was dead. Her owner, Glenda Stevens, was certain of it. Earlier in the day, she'd found the little dog's lifeless body sprawled across the road near the family's mailbox. Sweetie had been struck down by a delivery truck and her heart had stopped. Glenda was overcome with grief. She carried the limp body of the little dog to her backyard, dug a grave, and buried her.

Imagine Glenda's shock when hours later, she looked out of her back window and saw two hind legs sticking out of the ground. Sweetie was trying to dig her way out of her grave!

Glenda rushed to help her pet and then took her to the vet. The vet said the dog had a broken leg and a broken jaw and it would probably be best to put her to sleep. Glenda absolutely refused. Sweetie had already died once. Why make her go through that again?

Instead, she brought the dog to a specialist who was able to put Sweetie back together (just like in the movie *Frankenweenie*).

PETS OF THE FAMOUS (AND INFAMOUS)

If you ruled the world, what kind of pet would you have?

CLEOPATRA (69–30 B.C.). The queen of Egypt loved her cat, Charmian, so much that she designed her makeup to look like her cat's eyes.

KUBLAI KHAN (1215–1294). The Mongol emperor of China owned 5,000 mastiffs, the greatest number of dogs ever owned by one person.

NAPOLEON BONAPARTE (1769–1821). The emperor of France was deathly afraid of cats, but his wife Josephine had a pet orangutan that sat at her dinner table dressed in a coat.

PRESIDENT JOHN QUINCY ADAMS (1767–1848). He kept a pet alligator in the White House.

ADOLF HITLER (1889–1945). The Nazi dictator was scared of cats, but liked dogs. He had a German shepherd named Blondi that he trained to climb a ladder, jump through hoops, and sing.

DUMB ANIMAL TRICKS

Sometimes animals act just like humans…stupid.

OH, DEER!

The Storliens of Marietta, Minnesota, got the surprise of their life when they woke up one morning and found two "deer" lying in the front yard with their antlers locked together. One was a real deer, injured and struggling. The other was the Storliens' life-size concrete lawn ornament. Apparently the real deer spotted the fake deer during the night and challenged it to a duel. He charged, locked horns and knocked the lawn ornament over. Guess that showed him!

TRASH COMPACTOR

Did you hear about the bull terrier who swallowed a bottle cap, some Saran Wrap, a toy car, and some wire? The dog was rushed to the hospital, where doctors had to operate to remove the trash. In the recovery room the dog was put on an IV drip. When he woke up…he ate the IV tubing.

WHAT'S BLACK AND WHITE, BLACK AND WHITE, AND BLACK AND WHITE?

Answer: a herd of angry zebras kicking a minibus. The bus full of students was touring through a game park in Kenya when the enraged herd surrounded it and attacked. The driver finally got the kicking zebras to cool it by pouring bottles of water over the beasts' heads.

AND THE WINNER IS...

PICKIEST EATER. The Australian koala eats only eucalyptus leaves—and not from just *any* tree. It sorts through 500 species of eucalyptus to find one of the 36 types it likes. A pound and a half of eucalyptus leaves later, this fellow is full.

BIGGEST FARTER. The regular old farm cow blasts out more than 105 pounds of methane gas a year. Count all the cows around the globe and that adds up to billions of pounds of gas. Talk about air pollution!

FASTEST RUNNER. The cheetah wins the gold medal, paws down, reaching a top speed of 70 miles an hour. Run, Spot, run!

SLOWEST MOVER. The three-toed sloth of South America wins this award with a land speed of six to eight feet a minute.

BIGGEST SLEEPYHEAD. The koala again. It snoozes for 22 hours a day. But the two-toed sloth is a close second clocking 20 hours of z's a day.

SMALLEST MAMMAL. The Kitti's hog-nosed bat (also called the bumblebee bat) weighs a minuscule .07 ounces—about as much as a peanut!

DEADLIEST MAMMAL. Lion? Tiger? Cape buffalo? Hippo? Grizzly bear? Wrong on all counts. It's man.

WAGS TO RICHES

LUCKY DOG

Toby was a standard poodle who lived in a mansion in New York City. He slept on silk sheets on a miniature four-poster bed in his own bedroom. He even had a personal butler to serve his meals (his favorite: lamb chops). When his owner, Ella Wendel, died in 1931, she left her little darling $15 million. That's oodles for one poodle!

FAT CATS

When Dr. William Grier of San Diego, California, died, he left $415,000 to his 15-year-old cats Hellcat and Brownie. A third cat, Charlie Chan, got $250,000—all to himself.

STRONGHEART

Before there was a Lassie or an Air Bud,
he was the first great dog star.

In 1920 a Hollywood director and animal trainer named Lawrence Trimble discovered a German shepherd named Strongheart in Germany. Trimble took Strongheart home to try to turn him into a movie star.

Trimble was an unusual trainer. He didn't use treats as bribes to get Strongheart to perform. Instead, he read newspapers, books—even poetry—to the dog, and insisted that no one ever use baby talk with Strongheart or talk down to him. His training method was odd…but it worked.

At home Strongheart acted more like a human than a pet. He learned to help make his bed, arrange the furniture, put away his own toys, and even wash the car.

In 1921 he was ready for his first movie, *The Silent Call.* Strongheart became an instant star: thousands of fans would gather to see him when he toured the country. He made seven movies and was the biggest animal star of the 1920s. He even had a dog food named after him (it's still available today). Heading to Hollywood soon? Go to 1724 Vine Street. There you'll find a star on the Hollywood Walk of Fame…and all it says on it is "Strongheart."

ANIMAL CRACKERS

Two cows met in a field and started talking.

"Moo," said the first cow.

"I was just about to say the same thing!" said the second cow.

When his mother returned from the grocery store, little Jason pulled the box of animal crackers out of the bag and dumped them all over the kitchen counter.

"What on earth are you doing?" his mom asked.

"The box says you can't eat the cookies if the seal is broken," the boy explained. "I'm looking for the seal."

Q: How do you catch a runaway dog?
A: Hide behind a tree and make a noise like a bone!

Q: What do you call a chicken at the North Pole?
A: Lost.

Q: What is a twip?
A: A twip is what a wabbit takes when he wides on a twain.

Q: Why do cows wear bells?

A: Because their horns don't work.

S ome **kindergartners** were on the playground when a fire truck zoomed past. Sitting in the front seat of the fire truck was a Dalmatian. The children started arguing about the dog's duties.

"They use him to keep the crowds back," said one kid.

"No," said another, "he's just for good luck."

A third kid brought the argument to a close. "You're both wrong. They use the dog to find the fire hydrant."

BIG KAHUNA!

Hippos in West Africa have come up with a cool way to travel—they surf! Every evening the hippos of Loango National Park in Gabon come out of the jungle and ride the breakers down the beach to the grasslands for dinner. After eating as much as 150 pounds each, they surf back up the beach to their sleeping grounds.

Experts guess the hippos take to the ocean because floating in the surf takes a big load off their feet—the average hippo weighs about 6,000 pounds!

WILD AND WOOLLY FACT

Hippos look like they're sweating blood. That's because they secrete a sticky pink liquid to protect their sensitive skin. It doubles as a sunblock and moisturizer.

BIG MOUTH

DID YOU KNOW?

• A hippo's head can weigh 1,000 pounds.

• A four-foot-tall child can stand up inside a hippo's open mouth.

• A hippo's eye can see above and below the water at the same time.

• A hippo's skin is so thick ($1\frac{1}{2}$ inches) that most bullets can't penetrate it.

MOST DANGEROUS ANIMAL IN AFRICA

Every year more people in Africa are killed by hippos than by all other animals combined. They're particularly

dangerous in rivers, where they capsize boats. A hippo can run twice as fast as a human and can cut a crocodile in half with a single bite!

ROCK-A-BYE BABY

Shh! Some pretty incredible things are happening in the wild nursery.

ZEBRAS are born with brown stripes.

PORCUPINES are born with soft quills (lucky for Mama)! The quills start to harden an hour after birth.

CAMELS are born without humps.

ELEPHANT babies suck their trunks the way baby humans suck their thumbs.

POLAR BEAR babies weigh only about one pound, yet they can grow to weigh as much as a car.

GIANT PANDA babies are the size of a stick of butter when they're born.

KANGAROO babies are smaller than your finger. The inch-long baby, called a *joey*, must crawl to its mother's pouch, where it will continue to grow into a fully developed baby kangaroo.

MOM OF THE YEAR

Lions eat gazelles, right? Not Kamuniak, an unusual lioness living in Samburu National Park in Kenya.

In 2002 Kamuniak turned the natural order of the animal world upside down when she adopted a baby oryx. An oryx is a type of gazelle and is usually the favorite dish of lions and other predators. But Kamuniak, who had no cubs of her own, began to lick and clean the orphaned oryx calf like a newborn cub.

Worried rangers returned the calf to its mother. To their astonishment, Kamuniak promptly adopted another newborn oryx calf.

Kamuniak (which means "Blessed One" in the Samburu language) guards her calves from other lions and otherwise treats them like one of her own. So far she's adopted six in all. The baby gazelles stay with the lioness until they're strong enough to run away and rejoin their herd.

Meanwhile, Mama Kamuniak and her "babies" have become the most popular attraction at the game park, drawing visitors from all over the world.

SUPER DADS

Most baby animals are raised by their moms, but there are a few amazing dads in the animal kingdom.

TAMARINS win the title "Fathers of the Year," hands down. No other male animal takes care of its babies like these South American monkeys. Dad even helps Mom during labor. After the babies are born (she usual-

ly has identical twins), he gently washes the little ones and returns them to their mother. For the first few weeks Dad takes care of Mom while she tends the kids. Then Dad takes over full-time, teaching them everything they need to know to survive. But he's careful to return them to their mother every few hours for meals.

RED FOXES are great fathers, too. They bring food to Mama fox while she nurses. When the pups get older, Dad teaches them how to forage by hiding food. He teaches them how to fight by playing. And when it's time for them to leave home, Dad kicks them out. But just in case Junior isn't ready to be on his own yet, he always leaves some extra food just outside the den. Way to go, Dad!

RUN WITH THE PACK

There are some very creative names for groups of animals. Can you guess them?

What do you call
a group of **GIRAFFES**?
a. rise
b. tower
c. stand

Answer: **b.** tower

What do you call
a group of **TIGERS**?
a. ambush
b. growl
c. gang

Answer: **a.** ambush

What do you call
a group of **ZEBRAS**?
a. pattern
b. herd
c. dazzle

Answer: **c.** dazzle

What do you call a
group of **SQUIRRELS**?
a. scurry
b. scramble
c. run

Answer: **a.** scurry

What do you call
a group of **HIPPOS**?
a. blob
b. bloat
c. flotilla

Answer: **b.** bloat

What do you call
a group of **OTTERS**?
a. mischief
b. romp
c. giggle

Answer: **b.** romp

What do you call
a group of **RHINOS**?
a. army
b. platoon
c. crash

Answer: **c.** crash

What do you call
a group of **APES**?
a. meeting
b. shrewdness
c. mob

Answer: **b.** shrewdness

ANIMAL CRACKERS

An elephant was drinking from a river when he spotted a turtle asleep on a log. The elephant ambled over and kicked the unsuspecting turtle across the river.

"Why did you do that?" asked a passing giraffe.

"Because I recognized it as the same turtle that took a nip out of my trunk 47 years ago."

"Wow, what a memory!" said the giraffe.

"Yep," said the elephant. "Turtle recall."

Earl: I just bought a pet zebra.
Pearl: What are you going to name him?
Earl: Spot.

Q: What do you call a well-dressed lion?
A: A dandy lion (dandelion).

Q: How does an elephant get down from a tree?
A: He sits on a leaf and waits till autumn!

Q: What do you get if you cross a leopard with a plum?
A: A spotted purple people eater!

Q: What did the judge say when he saw the skunk in the courtroom?
A: "Odor in the court!"

ZOO STORIES

Monkey See... A chimp named Feili spent too many hours people-watching at the zoo in Zhengzhou, China, and picked up a human habit that's really hard to kick—smoking. For years, Feili smoked all the cigarettes she could find on the ground. When she ran out, she begged visitors for more. If they said no, Feili flew into a screeching rage and spit on them. Happily, Feili finally kicked the habit in 2005.

Big Is Beautiful. Maggie is a 22-year-old African elephant at the Alaska Zoo who's fighting the battle of the bulge. She weighs 9,120 pounds—that's 3,000 pounds more than the average female elephant. Even with daily walks around the zoo, Maggie couldn't shed those extra pounds. So the zoo built Maggie her very own treadmill. Now she gets up in the morning and works out, just like her zookeepers.

DUMB DOG TRICKS

TEED OFF

A Labrador retriever named Meatball had a monstrous stomachache and was rushed to the vet for an emergency operation. Meatball, who should have been named Meathead, lived near a golf course…and had scarfed down a record 23 golf balls!

BRAIN FREEZE

In January 1935, a collie was stranded on a piece of ice on Lake Michigan. Rescuers tried to coax the dog to safety but she wouldn't budge… until they offered her some pork chops. She promptly dove into the freezing water and swam to shore, where she ate the pork chops. Then she jumped back into the icy lake and swam back to her iceberg!

STUCK ON YOU

Dempsey the Doberman had to have his jaws separated after he ate an entire tube of superglue.

· FELIX THE CAT ·

Felix and his master, Thomas Lynan of St. Kilda, Australia, were inseparable. When the old man died, the black-and-white kitten was inconsolable. For five months, he hardly ate and spent his days and nights wandering the house looking for Mr. Lynan. Worried that Felix would die of grief, Lynan's daughter took the cat for a drive to cheer him up. When the car stopped at an intersection just outside of town, the cat, who had been lying limp in the backseat, suddenly leapt out the car window and ran off. The family searched everywhere for Felix but couldn't find him.

Days later, when Lynan's daughter went to visit her father's grave at Melbourne Cemetery ten miles away, she found Felix on the gravestone, marching back and forth like a sentry. She tried to take the cat home but he kept jumping out of the car and racing back to Lynan's grave. "In the end," she told a newspaper reporter, "we decided it would be kinder to let Felix stay behind."

Weeks later the reporter drove by the cemetery to see if Felix was still there. Sure enough, the black-and-white kitty was still standing guard over his master's grave.

HERE KITTY KITTY

A few cat facts to keep you feline fine.

MUMMY'S THE WORD

In ancient Egypt, cats were worshiped as gods. When they died, cats were mummified and taken to the temple of the cat god, Bastet. The Egyptians even mummified mice for the cats to take along as a snack in the afterworld.

DID YOU KNOW?

• A black cat is considered unlucky in America…but lucky in Great Britain.

• White cats with blue eyes are usually deaf.

MAMA CAT

The Weller family in Cranbook, British Columbia, woke up one morning to find their cat, Patches, nursing two baby mice. Patches already had seven kittens of her own. "I don't know where she found them," Mrs. Weller said, "but for some reason she brought them in instead of killing them." Good kitty.

LOOK OUT BELOW!

Gros Minou, a two-year-old orange-and-white cat from Quebec, holds the world record for surviving the longest fall. Gros Minou fell 200 feet off a 20th floor balcony into a flower bed. Amazingly, the lucky feline limped away with only a broken pelvis.

MISTER ED

A horse is a horse of course, of course, and no one can talk to a horse, of course. That is, of course, unless the horse is the famous Mr. Ed.

Mister Ed was a hit TV show in the 1960s that starred a "talking" horse named Mister Ed (his real name was Bamboo Harvester). This smart horse could do most of his own stunts, like opening the barn door and answering the telephone. What he *couldn't* do was talk. That was accomplished with a nylon bit which pulled his mouth open or by feeding him a peanut butter–like substance that made him chew.

Like many Hollywood stars, Ed could be difficult to work with. When he was tired, he'd just walk off the set. And when he got bored, he'd cross his back legs and yawn. When he was hungry, all shooting stopped while he strolled over to his bale of hay for a snack. That's star power!

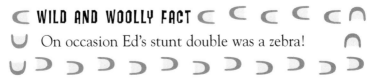

⊂ WILD AND WOOLLY FACT ⊂ ⊂ ⊂ ⊂ ⊂∩
∪ On occasion Ed's stunt double was a zebra! ∩
∪ ⊃ ⊃ ⊃ ⊃ ⊃ ⊃ ⊃ ⊃ ⊃ ⊃ ⊃

MORE RATS

ALL IN THE FAMILY

The San Carlos, California, health department got a call from horrified residents who reported seeing large rats eating the curtains in the window of a neighboring condo. Investigators found hundreds of rats running all over the house…even under the bedcovers. The owners's explanation: the rats were pets. "They have the bedrooms," the wife explained. "We sleep on the living room couch."

RAT TEMPLE

The Karni Mata temple in India is made of marble, gold, and silver. But it's known as the "Rat Temple." Why? It's home to about 20,000 rats who live there and

run free through the place. Hindu monks feed them bowls of milk and sweets, and some people even drink from the rats' bowls! (It's considered good luck.) Want to go? You can…but be warned: shoes are not allowed!

PEST CONTROL, IRISH STYLE

In ancient Ireland, people believed rats could be "rhymed to death." It was thought that hearing poetry would whip the rats into such a frenzy that they'd kill each other.

RAT TO THE RESCUE

A West Virginia coal miner became pals with a rat he found down in the mines. He shared his food with the rat and always made sure it was out of the way before he set off any explosions in the tunnel. One day the rat began to act strangely. It scurried back and forth in front of the miner, first running to him and then disappearing around the corner. The miner set down his tools and followed the rat. Just as he turned the corner, the tunnel collapsed—right on the spot the miner had been standing only seconds before!

PAMPERED PETS

We already have dog parks, dog toys, and doggy day care. What will they come up with next?

WHAT'S FOR DINNER?

At the Three Dog Bakery they're serving Drooly Dream Bars, pup tarts, and carob chip cookies. Sound good? Sorry—these tasty treats are for canine connoisseurs only. Gourmet dog treats are not just a passing fad; Three Dog Bakery has doggy diners throughout the United States, Canada, Japan, and Korea.

MEOW TV

At last! Television just for cats! Researchers say one third of all pet cats watch TV, so what could be better than *Meow TV?* This show brings shots of squirrels running up and down trees, inspirational programs about lions and tigers, and funny home videos of fellow felines right into your living room. *Purrfect!*

DOGS' DAY AT THE SPLASH

Hot dogs in Hutchinson, Kansas, get a chance to cool off on the last day of swim season at the Salt City Splash pool. People can go in the pool, too, but they have to stay in the shallow end. Dogs, however, can cannonball anywhere (and anyone) they like.

ANIMAL SIGNS

American Sign Language is a way to talk by using your hands. Can you match the sign with the animal's name?

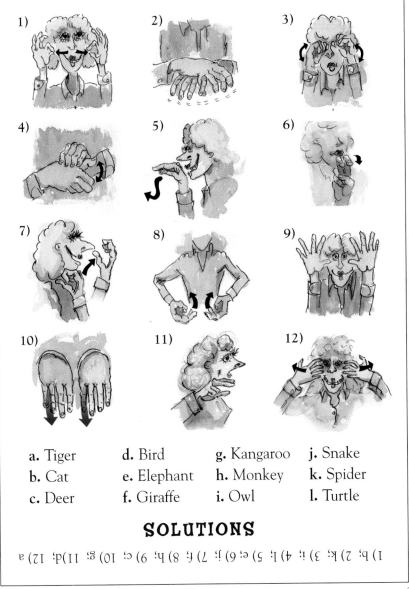

1)	2)	3)
4)	5)	6)
7)	8)	9)
10)	11)	12)

a. Tiger   d. Bird   g. Kangaroo   j. Snake

b. Cat   e. Elephant   h. Monkey   k. Spider

c. Deer   f. Giraffe   i. Owl   l. Turtle

SOLUTIONS

1) b; 2) k; 3) i; 4) l; 5) e; 6) j; 7) f; 8) h; 9) c; 10) g; 11) d; 12) a

WHAT ARE THEY?

MEERKATS!

DID YOU KNOW?

• Meerkats aren't cats—they're squirrel-sized mammals (related to the mongoose) that live in southern Africa.

• A meerkat's close-up vision is so bad that it often misses food that's right in front of it.

• When meerkats dig a tunnel, they form a line and pass dirt from one to the other, until it's out of the hole.

SUN WORSHIPPERS

When a meerkat gets chilly, it stands up on its hind feet and faces the sun. That's because the dark skin on its belly acts like a solar panel. The meerkat even has built-in sunglasses and windshield wipers. The dark band around its eyes reduces the harsh glare of the sun and, every time a meerkat blinks, a special membrane on the eye wipes away the sand.

LIFE IN THE MOB

Belonging to a mob is critical for a meerkat—it could never survive the African desert alone. The mob lives in an elaborate underground home that has nurseries, sleeping rooms, and even a common toilet. To keep the mob running smoothly, each meerkat has a specific job. There are hunters, teachers, babysitters, diggers, and guards.

WILD & WOOLLY FACT

Meerkats can close their ears to keep dirt and sand out while they are tunneling.

DING DONG!

One night Amelia Roybal of Albuquerque, New Mexico, answered her doorbell and discovered a very drunk monkey swaying on her doorstep. He staggered into the house, found her liquor cabinet, and poured himself a glass of whiskey. Amelia and her husband thought they were victims of a practical joke and

that someone was giving the monkey signals. But Myron the monkey was acting on his own.

After tossing back another shot of whiskey, Myron got belligerent and refused to give Mr. Roybal back the bottle. The Roybals called the sheriff, then cornered the monkey in the laundry room, where he promptly filled the washing machine full of soapsuds and flooded the room.

When the deputy sheriff arrived, he found Myron eating plastic fruit in the living room. Then Myron began hurling potatoes and oranges with dead-on accuracy at the Roybals and the deputy.

It took four more deputies and seven members of the Roybal family to capture the tipsy primate, but they finally did. It turned out Myron had escaped from a traveling circus. His trainer had started him drinking the hard stuff as a way to calm his nerves before performing. (Maybe somebody needs to train the trainer.)

AMAZING WORLD RECORDS

• **The Heaviest Dog.** Zorba, an English mastiff from London, tipped the scales at a whopping 343 pounds.

• **The Fattest Cat.** Himmy was a 46-pound tabby cat from Queensland, Australia, who was so chubby he had to be transported in a wheelbarrow.

• **The Oldest Dog.** Bluey was an Australian cattle dog who lived to the age of 29 years and 5 months.

WILD MEDICINE

Ever watch your dog eat grass when it's sick? It will sort through all the blades of grass to chew on the exact one that will give the best medicine. Other animals do the same thing.

CHIMPANZEES in Africa get rid of parasites by carefully folding the spiky leaves of the wild sunflower plant, rolling it around in their mouths and swallowing it whole. Chimps hate the taste of it—they make faces when they eat—but apparently they know it helps them.

AFRICAN ELEPHANTS in western Kenya risk their lives to get to a cave in Mount Elgon just to chew on the mineral-rich rocks there. The sodium in this extinct volcano is essential for their health.

CAPUCHIN MONKEYS of Costa Rica rub themselves with the Piper plant from the chili family to kill flies, ticks, and fleas and to numb the pain of insect bites.

RATS can't throw up. So when they're feeling sick, they eat clay—it absorbs the toxins in their stomachs.

GRIZZLY BEARS dig up the roots of the Loveroot plant (*Ligusticum porteri*), chew it to a pulp, and then rub the juices all over their faces and fur to treat stomachaches and bacterial infections.

PANDA-MONIUM

THE WEIGHTLIFTER

Ying Ying proves he is no "girly bear" during a performance in the Chinese Acrobats Arts Festival in Beijing. This 17-year-old is said to be the only panda who can lift weights, dunk a basketball, and drive a car.

BUFFALO PALS

Man's best friend comes in all shapes and sizes.

CHARLIE was a four-day-old orphan when he came to live with Roger Brooks and his wife, Veryl Goodnight, in Tesuque, New Mexico. Goodnight was a sculptor who needed a model for the buffalo piece she was working on. Charlie was a buffalo who needed a home.

In the beginning, Charlie was about the size of a golden retriever...and acted like one, too. He lived in the house, lounged on the sofa, and gave big wet kisses with his tongue. Even when he'd turned into a 200-pound bruiser, he tried to crawl into chairs with his owners.

"We weren't quite sure whether Charlie thought he was a human or whether he thought we were buffalo," Brooks says.

Being a buffalo, Charlie roamed wherever he pleased. Once he let himself into the house by walking through the screen door. He then marched up the stairs to the second floor and climbed into the king-sized bed in the master bedroom.

As Charlie got older, Brooks felt the 400-pound furry beast should spend a little more time outdoors, so he often took the buffalo for walks into the hills (or rather, Charlie took *him*). Brooks would follow Charlie and depending on the buffalo's mood, they'd stroll or just stand still. It was up to Charlie to decide. "The old saying about buffalo is that you find out where they want to be," Brooks explained, "and then you put the fence around them."

Charlie, who eventually topped the scales at 1,800 pounds, was finally weaned from his indoor home and went to live outdoors with two other tame buffalo on Brooks' ranch.

BUFFY THE WATER BUFFALO

has been living with her family, the Bellingers, on their ranch near Humpty Doo, Australia, for over 18 years. Like most teenagers, Buffy is always hungry, gets in trouble a lot, and is really hard on the family car. She likes to rub her head up against the car (which puts dents in the hood). She won't stay outside because she hates the rain, so she lives inside with the Bellingers.

Her worst habit? Pulling freshly washed clothes off the line and chewing them. Buffy loves the taste of laundry soap, which probably makes the Bellingers wish they never heard the song that goes, "Oh, give me a home where the buffalo roam…"

OLD MACDONALD HAD A...

HORSES breathe only through their nostrils.

Twelve or more **COWS** are known as a *flink*.

GOATS' eyes have rectangular pupils.

PIGS have four toes on each hoof but only two touch the ground.

SHEEP can recognize as many as 50 other sheep by sight.

PIGS are very clean. They always poop away from where they live.

MULES always lift their tails before they bray.

The underside of a **HORSE'S** hoof is called a *frog*.

SHEEP have a built-in instinct to follow the lead ram. If a ram jumps over a stick and you take away the stick, every sheep after the ram will jump over the place where the stick was.

DONKEYS' eyes are set in their heads so they can see all four feet at once.

FAINTING GOATS

This breed has bulging eyes and long, upright ears,
but otherwise they look and act like most goats.
Except for one teensy little problem...

When fainting goats are startled, their muscles stiffen and they fall over. The condition is called *myotonia*. It can be so extreme in some goats that even the noise of a passing car will make them keel over and faint. After 10 or 15 seconds, the goat gets up and walks away.

Shepherds used to keep fainting goats to protect their sheep. If a wolf attacked the herd, the goat would faint, which would attract the wolf and give the sheep a chance to escape. So who would protect the goat? Guess he was out of luck.

BOO!

THE NOSE KNOWS

POLAR BEARS can smell a seal on the ice 20 miles away. No wonder they're nicknamed "noses with legs."

ARCTIC HARES can smell dwarf willow leaves beneath several feet of snow.

SQUIRRELS can smell the tiny acorns they buried the previous autumn.

DOGS can smell one drop of urine in a swimming pool full of water.

WOLVES can smell prey more than a mile away if the wind is right. They can also smell the presence of an animal three days after it's gone.

PIGS can be trained to find truffles—prized edible fungi that grow underground. (Some police departments use pigs to sniff out drugs.)

COONHOUNDS can smell when a raccoon's track was made, how fast it was traveling, and in what direction.

BLOODHOUNDS can follow a scent that is four days old.

DOGS can point out a sick catfish to fish farmers and even smell if there are termites in the house.

UDDERLY RIDICULOUS

MOO-SIC LOVERS

The municipal band of Cortina d'Ampezzo, Italy, was marching through town one day when a herd of 25 cattle suddenly broke out of their pasture and deliberately butted the band members to the ground. Then, to everyone's surprise, the cattle stood around affectionately licking the instruments.

BEASTLY EXPRESSIONS

Where does Grandma come up with the crazy phrases she uses? Here are the origins of three of them.

DON'T LET 'EM GET YOUR GOAT.

Meaning: Don't let them upset you.

Story: Racehorses and other high-strung Thoroughbreds are sometimes given goats as stall-mates. The goats seem to calm the horses down, especially before a big race. At one time, crooks who were betting against a horse would steal its goat as a way to upset the horse and make it lose the race.

WHO LET THE CAT OUT OF THE BAG?

Meaning: Who revealed the secret?

Story: In medieval days, piglets were taken to markets and sold in sacks. Some crooks would stuff a cat into the bag and try to pass it off as a piglet. If the cat escaped in front of the potential buyer, so did the secret.

HE'S A STOOL PIGEON.

Meaning: He's a traitor.

Story: Pigeon hunters would use tame birds, tied to stools, to lure wild pigeons to come close and be caught.

AND THE WINNER IS...

⋃ The **LARGEST HORSE** on record: a Shire gelding named Samson. In 1850, at the age of four, Samson measured 7 feet 2 inches high (at the shoulder).

⋃ Samson was also the **HEAVIEST HORSE** on record. He weighed 3,360 pounds.

⋃ The **SMALLEST PONY** in history was a stallion named "Little Pumpkin." He stood 14 inches tall and weighed only 20 pounds.

⋃ The **OLDEST HORSE** on record: an English barge horse named "Old Bill." A horse's typical life span is 20 years. Bill was 62 when he died in 1802.

⋃ The **LONGEST TAIL** was on an American palomino named Chinook. It was 22 feet long.

⋃ The **LONGEST MANE** was 18 feet long and grown by a California mare named Maude.

⋃ The **FASTEST PONY EXPRESS RIDE** was 7 days, 17 hours—it was carrying President Lincoln's inaugural address.

ANIMAL NEWS
HAM ON THE LAM!

In 1998 two red-haired pigs escaped from a slaughterhouse in the town of Tamworth, England, by squeezing through a fence and swimming across the icy Avon River.

The British dubbed them "Butch Cassidy and the Sundance Pig" after the famous Wild West outlaws.

For the next six days TV crews and helicopters searched the countryside for the two escaped trotters.

The huge outpouring of support for the runaway piggies gave their owner a change of heart—he spared their lives and sold them to a London newspaper for the rumored sum of $24,500. The famous porkers were finally placed in an animal sanctuary and immortalized in a BBC television movie, *The Legend of the Tamworth Two.*

AND SPEAKING OF PIGS...

In the 1800s, families used to spend most of their money on a pig. Their pig acted as a garbage can by eating all the family's food scraps and also gave them pork, bacon, and sausage. When asked if he had any money, a farmer would reply, "No. All my money's in the pig." When people stopped keeping pigs they made a replica of their pig to put their money in. Hence the practice of saving money in a…

…PIGGY BANK.

ANINALS TO THE RESCUE

TRIXIE THE NURSE. Jack Fyfe of Sydney, Australia, lived alone, with only his border collie, Trixie, for company. So when he woke up one morning to discover he'd suffered a paralyzing stroke during the night, he thought he was a goner. He knew it might be days before anyone would find him. To his amazement, Trixie took care of him. The collie brought him water by soaking a towel in her water bowl and draping it over his face. After her bowl ran dry, Trixie soaked the towel in the toilet. The faithful dog kept Fyfe alive for nine days, staying by his side until his relatives finally found him and got him to a hospital.

CAT ATTACK. Bringing the family cat along on vacation saved two-year-old Janey Kraven's life. Janey was playing in front of her family's Adirondack Mountains cabin when a black bear seized her in its jaws and shook her like a rag doll. Jasper the cat sprang onto the bear's head and scratched at its eyes. The enraged bear let go of Janey and chased the cat into the woods. When Jasper came home two hours later, unharmed, he received a hero's welcome.

MAD COWS

PLANE SILLY

A British couple who left their antique airplane in a pasture while they went to lunch had a rude awakening when they returned. While they were chowing down at the local pub in Hereford, England, a herd of cows was enjoying their own meal: the airplane. Apparently the cows really liked the taste of the old canvas covering the vintage plane's metal frame. Those cows had expensive taste—their meal cost $15,000.

NIGHT-NIGHT

A farmer in Syracuse, New York, has discovered a way to keep his milk cows happy and producing lots of milk: water beds. John Marshman put several water beds in his barn…and the cows love sleeping on them. "Sometimes the cows stand in line and wait for a cow to leave," he said, "just so they can get in the same water bed."

GIRAFFE-A-MANIA

In 1827 a giraffe named Zarafa came to Paris as a gift to King Charles X. The French, most of whom had never seen such a creature, went wild for it, calling it "Sweet Thing." More than 100,000 people came to visit Zarafa and suddenly giraffe furniture, porcelain, and decorations were everywhere. Ladies wore gowns with themes like "Giraffe in love" and "Giraffe in exile." Men tied "giraffe knots" in their ties. Most bizarre was the "à la giraffe" hairdo. It was so tall that the women who wore it had to sit on the floor of their carriages when they went out to a ball.

DID YOU KNOW?

• An adult giraffe can easily look into a second story window.

• A giraffe's neck can be six feet long but has only seven bones—just like a human's.

• A giraffe can clean its ears with its tongue. (Can you?)

TALKING TREES

A giraffe's favorite food is the thorny acacia tree. It would strip a tree bare if the tree didn't have a clever way to stop the giraffe from overeating. Once the animal begins nibbling its leaves, the acacia tree broadcasts a warning—like a chemical SOS—to the rest of the tree to move a bitter-tasting chemical called *tannin* from its roots and branches into its leaves. The tannin makes the leaves taste terrible, even to a giraffe. But the giraffe can't just move on to another tree. The tree that was being munched on also warns nearby trees by sending a chemical warning into the air. Once the alarm is sounded, it takes less than

30 minutes for all of the trees in the grove to fill their leaves with tannin. The giraffes have learned that the best way to eat their favorite food is to just nibble a little bit and then move to another grove.

WILD AND WOOLLY FACT

The giraffe is one of the few animals born with horns. The horns lie flat against the skull when it is born and pop up during the giraffe's first week of life.

GOING APE!

Life behind bars made this gang go a little stir crazy.

In 1994 the baboons at the Emmen Zoo in Holland—all 120 of them—suddenly climbed into the trees in their compound and refused to come down. The zookeepers

were baffled. The hamadryas baboons normally spent most of their time on the ground, but now they would come out of the trees only for dinner, and even then, they'd grab the food and race back to the treetops to eat. This continued for three days. Then suddenly, they came out of the trees and acted as if nothing had happened. What caused their three-day climbing expedition? No one knows for sure…but it did coincide exactly with the collision of Jupiter and the comet Shoemaker-Levy.

WILD AND WOOLLY FACT

The ancient Egyptians considered hamadryas baboons to be the sacred attendants of Thoth, the scribe (writer) of the gods.

WASSUP?

Most animals can't talk, but hey, who needs words?

CHIMPANZEES greet each other by touching hands.

AN ADULT LION sends out messages with a roar that can be heard up to five miles away.

WHEN TWO DOGS approach each other, the dog that wags its tail slowly is the dominant dog.

ELEPHANTS "hear" super-low frequency calls from other elephants over a mile away through the bottoms of their feet.

CATS meow at humans but rarely at each other.

GORILLAS stick out their tongues when they're angry.

THE ONLY KIND OF DOG that can't bark is a basenji. It can, however, yodel.

AND THE WINNER IS...

TOP TEN LONGEST-LIVING LAND ANIMALS (AVERAGE LIFESPAN)

1. Box turtle (100 years)
2. Human (80)
3. African elephant (40)
4. Grizzly bear (25)
5. Horse (20)
6. Gorilla (20)
7. Polar bear (20)
8. White rhino (20)
9. Black bear (18)
10. Lion (15)

TOP FIVE HEAVIEST LAND MAMMALS (AVERAGE WEIGHT)

1. African elephant (16,500 lbs.)
2. Hippo (9,900 lbs.)
3. White rhino (8,000 lbs.)
4. Giraffe (4,200 lbs.)
5. Bison (2,200 lbs.)

TOP TEN DOG NAMES

1. Sam 2. Max
3. Lady 4. Bear
5. Buddy 6. Maggie
7. Bailey 8. Jake
9. Molly 10. Sadie

TOP FOUR FASTEST MAMMALS

1. Cheetah (71 mph)
2. Antelope (57 mph)
3. Wildebeest (50 mph)
4. Lion (50 mph)

THE GREAT ESCAPE

Never underestimate an animal's resourcefulness.

The plan was simple: first he'd paddle across the water-filled moat, using a log as a raft. Then he'd climb the cement wall, grab a bicycle, and pedal away. Unfortunately for Juan, a spectacled bear at the Berlin Zoo, the bicycle was chained to a bike rack and it wasn't going anywhere. But that didn't dampen Juan's fun. He ambled away from the bike and spent half an hour frolicking on the zoo's playground. While excited visitors snapped photos of Juan's Day Out, nervous zookeepers shot him with tranquilizers.

Though some parents were really concerned about their children's safety, the zoo's deputy director wasn't worried. "Spectacled bears eat both vegetables and meat," he said, "but children do not tend to be on their menu. I'd have been a lot more worried if one of our polar bears had escaped."

YOU BETTER RUN!

If a **STRIPED SKUNK** does a handstand...
Look out—it's spray time!

If a **GRIZZLY BEAR** stands on its hind legs and puffs its cheeks...
It's the grizzly way of saying, "My next meal is...you."

If a **MUSK OX** bows its head and presses its nose against its knee...
This action releases a smelly liquid from a gland in its nose (musk!) and means this ox is about to stomp on you.

If you hear a **LEOPARD** cough...
It's probably the last sound you'll ever hear, because that's what leopards do right before they pounce.

If a **CAPE BUFFALO** starts smashing bushes with its horns...
It's giving you a little demonstration of what it's going to do to your head.

If a **CHIMP** stops grinning at you...

Lips pressed together tightly means he's about to play a serious game of tag—and you're it.

If a **BLACK RHINO** starts bouncing around like it's had too much caffeine...

Here it comes—the animal equivalent of a runaway train.

If a **FEMALE LION** flicks her tail briskly from side to side while she stares at you...

Uh-oh. She's decided to have you for lunch.

If a **HIPPO** turns his butt toward you and starts wagging his tail like a windshield wiper...

He's about to give you a dung shower—that's the male hippo's messy but oh, so effective way of marking his territory.

LOOK WHO'S TALKING

Match the animal with its sound.

1. bear 1	a. gibbers 4
2. fox 2	b. snorts 8
3. giraffe 3	c. barks 2
4. ape 4	d. roars 6
5. hippopotamus 5	e. trumpets 7
6. lion 6	f. howls 9
7. elephant 7	g. bellows 10
8. rhinoceros 8	h. bleats 3
9. wolf 9	i. growls 1
10. bull 10	j. brays 5

ANSWERS

1-i (bears growl); **2-c** (foxes bark); **3-h** (giraffes bleat); **4-a** (apes gibber); **5-j** (hippos bray); **6-d** (lions roar); **7-e** (elephants trumpet); **8-b** (rhinos snort); **9-f** (wolves howl); **10-g** (bulls bellow).

ROYAL RIDES

THE GREAT HORSE

Alexander the Great conquered most of the known world (Europe and Asia) in the 4th century B.C. According to legend, he always rode into battle astride his black stallion, Bucephalus. Alexander's father had owned the horse but could never tame it. Ten-year-old Alexander realized that the horse was afraid of its own shadow, so he turned Bucephalus to face the sun. Once it couldn't see its shadow, it relaxed, and Alexander began to train it. Together, the duo traveled 11,000 miles in eight years. When Bucephalus died at the age of 30, Alexander named a town in Pakistan in his horse's honor.

NO HORSE SENSE

The Roman emperor **Caligula** (A.D. 12 – 41) had a horse named Incitatus who lived in a marble stable with an ivory stall and purple blankets. Incitatus often wore a jeweled collar and had his own house with furniture and slaves.

HORSE SHOES?

Julius Caesar's favorite horse had hooves that looked like human feet. Each hoof was split in five parts that resembled toes. When the colt was born, soothsayers predicted, "The master of this horse will one day rule the world." Caesar made sure he became the master.

✚ ANIMALS TO THE RESCUE ✚

BACKSEAT DRIVER

A schnauzer named Bitsy was in the passenger seat when her owner suffered a heart attack while speeding down a Texas freeway. Bitsy quickly turned the wheel so the car would leave the road and then bit her owner, Jesus Martinez, until his foot came off the accelerator. The car stopped safely on the side of the road and Martinez recovered in the hospital.

CALL 911

Lyric the Irish setter was trained to help Judy Bayly, who had asthma. Once when Bayly's oxygen mask fell off during an asthma attack, Lyric knocked the phone off the hook and actually dialed the emergency number, saving Bayly's life.

GOOD DOGGIE!

FOREVER FAITHFUL

A bronze statue in Togliatti, Russia, honors the memory of a remarkably loyal German shepherd. When his owners were killed in a car crash, Faithful refused to move from the spot where they died. Townspeople brought Faithful food and water and tried to coax him into their homes, but the dog lived up to his name. He remained faithful to his owners until he died seven years later of old age.

BREEDS APART

Newfoundland dogs are strong swimmers. Why? They have webbed feet.

The greyhound has the best eyesight of any dog breed.

Great Danes can eat up to $8\frac{1}{2}$ pounds of food a day.

Chinese crested dogs can get acne.

HOW OLD IS YOUR DOG?

Want to figure out your dog's true age in people years?

1. Count the first full year as 15 years.
2. Count the second full year as 10 years.
3. Count all of the following years as 3 years apiece.

So a 5-year-old dog would be:
15 + 10 + 3 + 3 + 3 = 34 years old

RAILROAD JACK

*One of South Africa's most famous signalmen
wasn't a man—he was a baboon.*

In 1877 a railroad worker in South Africa named
James Wide accidentally fell under a train and lost
both of his legs. Without the use of his legs he could no
longer work on the trains, so he became a signalman at
Uitenhage Station near Port Elizabeth. His job: using a
system of flags and flashing lights to signal trains to slow
down or stop. Then he would pull a lever to transfer
them to different tracks.

Wide lived all alone near the station, struggling to
get around on peg legs and crutches. One day he saw a
trained baboon named Jack at a market in Uitenhage.

Hoping the baboon might help him, Wide brought Jack home and they soon became fast friends. As time passed, Jack began to do chores around the house: pumping water, doing dishes, and working in the garden. Soon the baboon learned to help Wide at the railroad station, too.

Locomotive drivers would blow four whistle blasts when they needed coal. Wide would hobble out on his crutches and hand them the key to the coal shed. One day Jack the baboon heard the whistle...and immediately raced to give the key to the locomotive driver. Soon, Jack was not only delivering keys but also giving the signals to the engineers and pulling the levers to switch the tracks. Jack did his job so well that the government gave him an employment number and a monthly paycheck.

"Jack the Signalman" worked at his job for 13 years... and never made a single mistake.

OTHER WORKING ANIMALS

ASTRONAUT: Laika was the world's first space traveler. Russian scientists shot the small dog into orbit in a satellite called Sputnik II on November 3, 1957.

GUIDE DOG: The first guide dogs—German shepherds— were trained by the German government to assist blind war veterans at the end of World War I.

LAB ASSISTANT: Rats' keen sense of smell can detect diseases like tuberculosis and bladder cancer in laboratory samples. A rat can diagnose up to 2,000 lab samples a day; a human (using a microscope) can only diagnose 20.

'ROO

You'll find these critters in Australia.

DID YOU KNOW?

 There are 45 kinds of kangaroos, including wallabies, walleroos, and pademelons.

 Male kangaroos are called *boomers*; females are *flyers*.

 If you lift a kangaroo's tail off the ground it can't jump.

 Kangaroos can go for months without water.

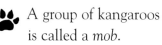 A group of kangaroos is called a *mob*.

1-2 PUNCH

Kangaroos really do punch at each other when they fight. One prizefighting kangaroo escaped from a Japanese zoo and knocked out three men before two policemen who knew judo finally stopped him.

THE ONE-EYED KANGAROO

The true story of an Australian hero.

In 1993 Lulu the kangaroo was found wounded in the pouch of her mother, who'd been killed by a car. The Richards family adopted the one-eyed western gray, and she quickly became one of the family, acting more like a dog than a kangaroo. As Mr. Richards worked around his ranch, Lulu was always at his side.

While he was out inspecting damage from a bad storm, a branch fell on Richards and knocked him out. Lulu immediately tried to alert the family. Standing guard over the injured man, she barked like a dog until the family came running out to see what was wrong.

According to Richards, "If it wasn't for Lulu, I'd be pushing up daisies." Her behavior was so extraordinary that Lulu became the first native animal to receive Australia's National Animal Valor Award.

ANIMAL CRACKERS

One day an arctic explorer came face to face with a polar bear. Afraid of being eaten, he fell to his knees and started praying. When the bear knelt down beside him and started praying too, the man shouted, "It's a miracle! I'm saved!"

The polar bear opened one eye and said, "Shh! Please don't talk while I'm saying grace."

What do you get if you cross a flea with a rabbit?
Bugs Bunny.

How do you stop a skunk from smelling?
Hold its nose.

What do you get from a cow at the North Pole?
Ice cream.

Why do mother kangaroos hate rainy days?
Because the kids have to play inside.

What do you call a flying ape?
A hot-air baboon.

What kind of beans do llamas like to eat?
Llima beans.

Q: WHAT IS IT???

Its nose is billed like a duck's.

 It lays eggs like a chicken.

It has poisonous venom like a snake.

 It has sharp claws for digging like a mole.

It has waterproof fur like a seal.

 It has a flat tail like a beaver.

Its feet are webbed like an otter's.

When the first specimens of this Australian mammal were brought to England in 1798, the British thought it was a fake. What is it?

Answer on the next page.

A: IT'S A PLATYPUS!

As odd as it looks, the duck-billed platypus is perfectly suited to live underwater and underground.

The bill. The platypus's bill isn't hard like a bird's beak—it's made of soft cartilage, like your nose or ears. The bill is lined with tiny sensors that help the platypus find food in dark places.

Babies. The duck-billed platypus lays eggs. Each egg is less than an inch long and sticks to the fur on the mother's belly. The babies, called *platypups*, hatch  after ten days and stay stuck to their mom until they are three to four months old. Only two other mammals lay eggs (they're both in the anteater family).

Claws. When the male platypus is attacked it protects itself by clawing at its enemy with the spurs on its hind legs. Those spurs really pack a punch—they're filled with poisonous venom that's strong enough to kill a dog.

Habitat. You can find this weird and wonderful beast along the banks of freshwater rivers and lakes in Eastern Australia.

MORE ZOO STORIES

Hey! Stop monkeying around!

SLIP AND SLIDE

At the Oklahoma Zoo the keepers had just finished mopping the floor of the orangutan's cage when the ape, who was sulking in the corner, stood up with his hands out, palms down, took a running start, and slid across the floor, as if he were surfing.

PLAYING WITH BONGO

It seems there's a practical joker in every crowd, even at the Sacramento Zoo. When Brigette, a slightly pudgy gorilla, got stuck in a rubber tub in her cage, her mate Bongo rushed to her side—not to help her, but to tickle her. As Brigette struggled to get out of the tub and away from his tickling, Bongo and their son Fossey collapsed on the floor in laughter.

GOING APE

Zippy was a spirited chimp from New Orleans who decided to sneak out of his owner's house and have a night on the town. Hours later, the police found him riding around in a van with four teenagers. The teenagers said they'd found Zippy outside a convenience store. He was wearing tennis shoes and blue underwear, and smoking a cigar.

HOLLYWOOD HOUNDS

LASSIE starred in nine movies, a radio show that lasted six years, and a TV series that ran for 19 years.

Lassie is supposed to be a girl, but all of the dogs who have played her were males.

There have been nine Lassies.

The original Lassie was named Pal. He made seven *Lassie* movies from 1947 to 1951, and starred in the first TV episode of *Lassie* at the age of 14.

BENJI'S real name was Higgins. He got his start in the '60s TV show *Petticoat Junction* and came out of retirement at age 14 to star in the Benji movies.

TOTO in *The Wizard of Oz* was a cairn terrier named Terry. He got the part because he looked just like the dog in the pictures from the book.

RIN TIN TIN had been rejected by every studio in Hollywood when Warner Bros., a studio that was about to go broke, took a chance on him in 1922. The success of his movies saved the studio.

FRAIDY PIGGY

Ever wonder what's hiding under the bed or in the closet? It probably never occurred to you to wonder what's going to come in through the back door.

An elderly couple in Minden, Germany, had just settled in for the night when a wild boar crashed through their patio door and jumped in bed with them. "I thought a bomb had dropped," said Andreas Janik, 71. "I sat up and there was a wild pig in bed, tusks and all." The pig was being chased by a neighbor's Yorkshire terrier. The Janiks had to chase the dog off before they could get the pig to leave. "I can't believe it was afraid of such a little dog."

I VANT TO SUCK YOUR BLOOD!

VAMPIRE BATS aren't dangerous to people.
However, if you're a cow, a pig, or a horse—look out.
These three-inch-long bats attack while their victims
are asleep. They land near the animal, then crawl
over the ground and try to find a furless part of the
body, like an ankle or the neck. Finally they make
a small slit-like wound in the animal and suck out
the blood. A vampire bat drinks more than
its own weight in blood every night.

GHOST PETS

Man's best friend is a...ghost?

PET CEMETERY

If late one night you happen to be passing the Hollywood Cemetery in Richmond, Virginia, stop and listen closely. You might hear the happy barks of ghost pets scampering around their owner's grave. The people of Richmond say they belong to author Ellen Glasgow who left orders to have her dogs exhumed from her backyard and buried with her when she died.

GHOSTLY WARNING

Norma Kresgal was sound asleep in her home in New York when the barking of her collie, Corky, suddenly awakened her. But that wasn't possible. Corky was dead! Yet his warning was so vivid that she got up to see what was the matter and discovered that her house was on fire. Her dead pet had saved her life.

NOW YOU SEE HIM, NOW YOU DON'T

At King John's Hunting Lodge in Somerset, England, a tabby cat enters a wood-paneled room through a closed door, curls up happily on the rug, and then...disappears.

THE BEAR FACTS

How can such a fierce creature be so cute?
Fortunately, you'll never bump into a polar
bear...unless you live near the North
Pole (or go to the zoo).

DID YOU KNOW?

• A polar bear is the only mammal with hair on the soles of its feet.

• Polar bears are the tallest bears (10 feet).

• All polar bears are left-handed.

• Polar bears don't drink water.

WHITE OUT

Polar bears are white, right? Wrong. A polar bear's fur is made of hollow, colorless hairs that transmit ultraviolet rays to the bear's skin and reflect the light. This makes for great camouflage. When a polar bear stalks its prey, it hides its black nose with its paw or covers it in snow so it will completely blend in with its environment.

It doesn't always work out, though. At the San Diego Zoo, three polar bears turned green when an algae colony moved into their hair shafts. Zookeepers brought back their white appearance with a little water and a lot of salt.

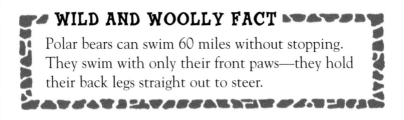

WILD AND WOOLLY FACT

Polar bears can swim 60 miles without stopping. They swim with only their front paws—they hold their back legs straight out to steer.

FROZEN FOODS

*Cool food facts from the
far, frozen North.*

BEAR SHARE

• The Siberian brown bear eats only fish heads and
throws away the bodies.

• The Siberian white-breasted bear eats only the fish
bodies and throws away the heads.

OFF WITH THEIR HEADS!

The Arctic fox bites the heads off birds
before burying them for
their winter reserves.

ARCTIC
ANTI-FREEZE

Most animals don't
eat moss because it's
hard to digest and has
little nutritional value.
But reindeer love it.
Why? It has a special
chemical that keeps the
reindeer's body fluids from
freezing, just like
antifreeze keeps water
in cars from freezing.

Q: WHY DON'T POLAR BEARS EAT PENGUINS?

A: Penguins live in the Southern Hemisphere—Antarctica, Australia, New Zealand, and South America. But polar bears live only in the Northern Hemisphere—northern Canada, Russia, and the Arctic Circle.

HISTORY MAKERS

It's reigning cats and dogs!

KING CANINE. In the 11th century, the king of Norway took revenge on his subjects—who had once ousted him—by putting his dog, Saur, on the throne. The dog reigned for three years.

CAT-ASTROPHE. The Battle of Agincourt (1415) was one of England's greatest triumphs. Led by King Henry V, the English defeated a much larger French army. How? They brought cats into battle to keep rats away from their food, but the French didn't. Legend has it that the night before the big battle, rats got into the French armory and gnawed through the archers' bow-strings. When the battle was fought, the French had no arrow power and King Henry—and his cats—won.

DOG EXPLORES AMERICA. From 1803 to 1806, explorers Lewis and Clark mapped the western United States with the help of Seaman, a 150-pound Newfoundland. The pooch was a respected member of the expedition team who warned them of charging buffalo and bears. His adventures were reported in the explorers' diaries and in the book *The Captain's Dog*.

BIG SCAREDY-CAT. The ancient Greek conqueror Alexander the Great was so afraid of cats that he would faint at the sight of one.

LION TALES

Knights of old often put images of lions on their shields and flags. Every pose had a French name, because French was the language of chivalry.

1. *Lion rampant* (raised forepaws)
2. *Lion statant guardant* (standing, full face)
3. *Lion rampant guardant* (raised forepaws, full face)
4. *Lion passant* (walking, right leg raised)
5. *Lion statant* (standing)
6. *Lion passant guardant* (walking, full face)
7. *Lion sejant* (sitting)
8. *Lion sejant rampant* (sitting up on forelegs)
9. *Lion couchant* (lying down)
10. *Lion salient* (leaping)
11. *Lion coward* (tail between legs)
12. *Lion queue fourchée* (double tailed)

NAME THAT HORSE

APPALOOSA. This type of spotted horse, first bred

by the Nez Perce tribe in Oregon and Washington, was originally called "a Palouse horse" after the Palouse River. That became "a Palousey," then "Appaloosey," and finally, Appaloosa.

MORGAN. As partial payment of a debt, in 1790 a one-year-old colt was given to a Vermont schoolteacher named Justin Morgan. The colt was the founding sire of the Morgan breed—pony-sized with large eyes and a white stripe down the center of the face.

CLYDESDALE. These large draft horses (horses used for pulling heavy loads) with fringed hooves were named after Scotland's Clydesdale district. They are probably best known as the team that pulls the Budweiser

beer wagon in TV commercials and parades.

PERCHERON. In 1823 a horse named Jean Le Blanc was born in the Perche region of France, and all of today's Percheron bloodlines trace directly to this horse. Originally the Percheron were used to carry knights into battle; now they are draft animals.

LIPIZZAN. In 1580 Archduke Charles II of Austria established a stud farm in Lipizza (now known as Lipica, Slovenia). He imported the best Spanish, Andalusian, Barbs, and Berber horses and bred them with the local Karst horse. The result is the famous leaping white Lipizzan stallions.

MUSTANG. The Spanish brought these horses to Mexico in the 16th century, but many of them escaped and headed north. They soon formed herds and roamed the western plains of the United States. The word *mustang* comes from the Spanish *mesteno* which means "stray or riderless horse."

ARABIAN. Considered by many horse lovers to be the finest breed, the Arabian has been bred for centuries by the Bedouin people of Syria, Iran, Iraq, and the Arabian peninsula.

WILD AND WOOLLY FACT

The smallest horse breed is the Falabella—a miniature from Argentina. The tallest of the breed stands less than 34 inches at the shoulder.

ANIMAL NEWS

CATS PREDICT EARTHQUAKE!

According to James P. Berkland, a geologist from California, there are many ways to predict earthquakes. When he predicted the 1989 Loma Prieta quake, he studied the tides and positions of the sun and moon. But he also studied the number of lost cat ads in the local papers. After ten full years of scientific observation, Berkland concluded that "cats tend to vanish just before a major tremor."

Is he right? In 1976 the people in the northern Italian village of Friuli noticed that their cats were acting strangely. Many of them were running around scratching on doors and howling to get out. Once out, they raced to get out of town. Three hours later the area was hit by a major earthquake.

WAR HEROES

They're trained to recognize booby traps and land mines, warn troops of ambushes, and even sacrifice their lives to save their "fellow soldiers."

CHIPS

When this U.S. Army dog and his handler, Private John Rowell, landed in Sicily in 1943, they were pinned down on the beach by a hail of machine-gun fire from an enemy bunker. Then Chips, a German shepherd–husky mix,

shook off his leash and charged. The enemy soldiers sprayed bullets at the attacking dog, nicking his shoulder and putting one in his hip. But nothing stopped Chips. He tore into the bunker and, moments later, four terrified enemy soldiers surrendered. One of them still had Chips clamped solidly onto his neck. Chips was awarded the Silver Star for bravery and a Purple Heart for wounds received in action. Disney even made a TV movie about Chips in 1990, called *Chips the War Dog*.

GANDER

This Newfoundland dog fought with Canadian troops against the Japanese during World War II. During a fierce battle on Christmas Eve in 1941, some Canadian soldiers lay wounded on the field when the enemy lobbed a live grenade at them. Gander picked up the grenade and carried it away. The dog was killed instantly when it exploded. "Was it a dog playing a dog game? I don't think so," said Jeremy Swanson of the Canadian War Museum. "Gander had seen many grenades explode in the days leading up to that moment. He saw something dangerous and took it away from his friends." Gander received the Silver Medal for bravery under fire.

SORTER

Two thousand years ago in ancient Greece, invaders used the cover of darkness to mount a sneak attack on the citadel of Corinth. What the attackers didn't know was that the Corinthians had set 50 watchdogs on guard along the seashore. When the invaders stepped out of their boats, the dogs set on them like lions. The outnumbered dogs fought bravely until all were killed but one—Sorter. He ran back into town, barking a warning that gave the Corinthians time to mount a defense and repel the invaders. The people were so grateful that they raised a monument to honor Sorter and the 49 loyal dogs who died that day.

DUMB DOG TRICKS

BAD HAIR DAY

The police were called in when a French woman's guard dog refused to let her into her own home. She'd gone to the beauty parlor and her new hairdo changed her looks so much that the dog didn't recognize her.

MOBILE MEAL

What do you do when you can't find your cell phone? Dial the number and listen for the ring. That's what a gas station attendant in Turkey did…and was shocked to hear his dog's stomach ringing! Apparently his pup had swallowed his Nokia.

ANIMALS TO THE RESCUE

✚ ✚

BABY ON BOARD

A woman in Raducaneni, Romania, nearly fainted when her sheepdog came home with a newborn baby. She was afraid the pooch, Vasile, had stolen the child from someone's home. But actually, Vasile had found the baby abandoned in a field two miles away. The dog carried the child home in his mouth, then barked and scratched at the door until someone came to help.

HEAD 'EM UP

In 1996 a farmer in Carmarthen, Wales, was tending a sick calf when a neighbor's bull attacked him. The bull beat Donald Mottram senseless, stomping on his head and body until he lost consciousness. When he came to later, he found that his cows had formed a protective circle around him. Led by Daisy, the "bell cow" of the herd, the cows kept up an impenetrable shield against the raging bull, which charged them over and over but never broke through their ranks. Finally the farmer was able to crawl for help. When asked to explain why his cows came to his defense, Mottram said, "I have always treated the animals reasonably and in return, they have looked after me."

WHO LET THE DOGS OUT?

They're in the air, on the road, and in the water.
There ain't nothing like these hound dogs.

BOARDER BULLDOG

Tyson is an English bulldog from Huntington Beach, California, who loves to skateboard. This major boarder taught himself how to skate when he was just one year old. He runs with three paws on the road and steers with his fourth paw on the skateboard. When Tyson gets going fast enough, he hops on the board and skates like a pro.

SURF DOG

Apache is a surf hound from Maui, Hawaii. This golden retriever started out tandem surfing with former surf champion Nancy Emerson. Now Apache does stunts on her own custom surfboard. She also helps to inspire the beginning surfers who paddle out with the Nancy Emerson School of Surfing. As Nancy says, "If my dog can surf, so can you."

*   *   *

A NAME GAME

Some animals have many names. Can you guess them?

1) A **mountain lion** is also...
  a. a puma
  b. a cougar
  c. a catamount
  d. all of the above

2) A **panther** is also...
  a. a tiger
  b. a leopard
  c. a lion
  d. all of the above

ANSWERS

1) d. All of the above; 2) b. Panthers are leopards without spots.

93

VIP'S VIPS
(VERY IMPORTANT PEOPLE'S VERY IMPORTANT PETS)

Florence Nightingale, the famous British nurse known as "the Lady of the Lamp," kept 60 Persian cats in her home and carried a tiny pet owl named Athena in her pocket when she cared for patients during the Crimean War in 1854.

Lucy Hayes, wife of U.S. President Rutherford B. Hayes, was the first American to own Siamese cats. They were a gift from the American consul in Siam (now Thailand), hence the name Siamese.

Pablo Picasso, the Spanish painter, owned an Afghan hound called Kasbec. He also owned a painting done by a chimpanzee.

Sir Isaac Newton, the British physicist from the 1600s, considered one of the most influential scientists of all time, was a cat owner. In addition to discovering gravity, he also invented the cat door.

MORRIS
THE CAT

The year was 1968. Morris the Cat was moments away from execution in a Chicago animal shelter when animal handler Bob Martwick spotted him and saw right away that this tabby cat had star quality. He took Morris from the shelter, straight to Hollywood. Soon the 9Lives cat food company made Morris the "finicky eater" star of their TV commercials. Morris became the darling of the talk-show circuit, starring in the movie *Shamus* with Burt Reynolds, hosting his own TV special, and even "co-authoring" three books on cat care. But the tough tabby from Chicago never forgot his roots—he toured the country promoting responsible pet adoptions, pet care, and his favorite food, 9Lives. The company donated millions of dollars in cat food and cash to shelters across the United States. The original Morris died in 1979 but his successors (the current Morris is Number 4) carry on his legend. His picture still hangs on the wall of the Chicago shelter where the greatest cat star of all time was first discovered.

CATTLE CALL

Did you know you can lead a cow upstairs but not down? Here are more quirky bovine facts.

EW, GROSS!

Cows clean their noses with their tongues.

YOU RANG?

Some Japanese farmers have a modern way to let their cows know when it's chow time: pagers. They hang one around each cow's neck. At dinnertime, the beeper goes off and the cows head for the trough.

BEST-DRESSED COWS

British farmers dress their cows in colorfully striped leggings, but not because they want them to be fashionable. It's so drivers can see the cows more easily at night.

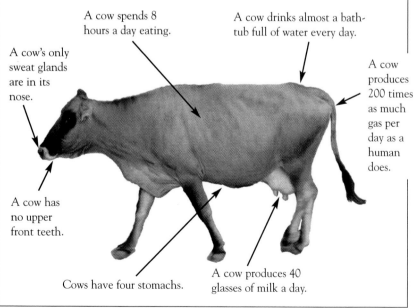

A cow spends 8 hours a day eating.

A cow drinks almost a bathtub full of water every day.

A cow's only sweat glands are in its nose.

A cow produces 200 times as much gas per day as a human does.

A cow has no upper front teeth.

Cows have four stomachs.

A cow produces 40 glasses of milk a day.

SOME PIG!

It's official: Pigs are the smartest animals on the farm.

GAME BOYS

Pigs do tricks, respond to verbal commands, and even play computer games. In one study some porkers used their snouts to move the joystick to shoot at targets and had a hit rate of 80 percent.

NO SWEAT

Did you ever hear the phrase "sweat like a pig"? Guess what? Pigs can't sweat! They don't have sweat glands.

MR. PIG HOGS IT ALL!

A pet porker named Mr. Pig and a dog named Calamity Jane inherited $600,000 when their owner, Margo Lamp, died in 1990. When the dog died, Mr. Pig became the sole inheritor. (Did he keep the money in his piggy bank?)

POODLE DOO

Poodles are smart, strong, fast, and loyal.
So, what's with that wacky hairdo?

Originally, the poodle cut had a practical purpose. The fur was kept thick around the joints and organs for protection in cold water. The rest of its coat was shorn to keep it from getting caught in the brambles. Then, somewhere around the 1700s, owners went a little nutty. Groomers clipped the dogs in any design their owners requested, such as a family coat of arms or monograms. They even sported tiny mustaches and pointy beards. Often they capped the poodle with a pompadour to match the owner's big puffy wig. Poodles were a natural for the circus—smart and talented—and their exaggerated pom-poms matched the round pompoms on the clowns' costumes.

TELE-CUBBY. A Beauséjour, Canada, teenager was startled to find a bear in his basement, lounging in front of the fireplace, eating potato chips, and watching TV.

COUCH POTATO. A family in Evesham, England, discovered a ferret on their couch, cheerfully watching their telly.

IT'S A HOOT. An owl in Jiangxi, China, loved TV so much that he built his nest in the rafters of one family's home. The owl slept during the day and watched TV from the kitchen table all night.

APE TV. Gorillas at the Moscow Zoo were getting so bored that televisions were installed in their cages. The zoo director said, "We want them to spend less time picking their noses and more time thinking about life."

SMARTY JONES

At the 2004 Kentucky Derby, a little chestnut colt named Smarty Jones won the hearts of Americans because of his champion spirit and his amazing story.

SOMEDAY FARM

Things started out nicely for Smarty. He was born at Someday Farm in New Hope, Pennsylvania, on February 28, 2001. Smarty's owners, Roy and Pat Chapman, wanted to name the spunky colt after Pat's mother, Mildred McNair (who was also born on February 28). But they didn't think "Mildred" was a very good name for a racehorse...so they gave him Mildred's nickname, "Smarty Jones."

DISASTER STRIKES

Nine months later, the Chapmans' horse trainer and his wife were murdered. The shock was so great to the Chapmans that they decided to sell the farm and most of their horses, including Smarty. But on the day of the sale the little horse hid out in the pasture with his mother, so they kept him.

DISASTER STRIKES AGAIN

The Chapmans sent Smarty to a trainer named John Servis in Philadelphia. But tragedy struck again when Smarty reared up and hit his head on an iron bar in the starting gate and collapsed, unconscious. Smarty hit his head so hard he fractured his skull and shattered his eye socket. John Servis thought Smarty had killed himself. Miraculously Smarty lived, but he nearly lost his left eye.

THE COMEBACK KID

After weeks in the hospital and a month of rest, Smarty Jones went back into training. His jockey was a Canadian named Stewart Elliot. Elliot had won thousands of races but had never ridden in the Kentucky Derby. Some

thought of that as a drawback, but it turned out that the partnership between "Stew" Elliot and Smarty Jones was a good one. Smarty won his first eight races—at eight different distances and at five different tracks.

This little champion was making such a splash on the racing scene that one man told the Chapmans to name their price and he'd pay it. Any amount! The Chapmans nearly sold Smarty for millions, but they decided to hold out to see if he could win the Kentucky Derby. They weren't disappointed.

THE WINNER'S CIRCLE

On May 4, 2004, the undersized Thoroughbred with the dent still showing in his head was first across the finish line at the Kentucky Derby. Less than two weeks later, Smarty Jones won the Preakness Stakes and became the first horse in 27 years to win both races.

🐾　🐾　🐾

RANDOM DOG FACTS

- All dogs are descendants of wolves.

- Dogs sweat through the pads of their feet, not by panting.

- A dog's nose print is like a human fingerprint—no two are alike.

- Nine mail carriers a day are bitten by dogs.

HORSE PUCKY

Here's the inside poop on life in the theater.

A TRUE STORY

In a production of *Camelot* in the 1970s, a horse had to appear on stage every night. To make sure that the horse didn't poop on the stage and embarrass everyone, a veterinarian was hired to put his hand up the horse's butt and pull out any waste before the horse appeared on stage. One night, just before the cue, the veterinarian was doing his job when the horse tightened his muscles and the vet's arm got stuck. The cue came and the horse made his entrance—with a man sticking out of his butt!

BEASTLY EXPRESSIONS

More origins of the crazy phrases you may have heard Grandma say.

NEVER LOOK A GIFT HORSE IN THE MOUTH.

Meaning: When you get a gift, don't question it—just accept it with gratitude.

Story: You can tell the age of a horse by looking at its teeth. Checking his age is sort of like looking for the price tag on a gift—you could be in for a big shock.

I SMELL A RAT!

Meaning: Something is terribly wrong.

Story: In the olden days, rats often lived quietly in the walls of houses. People didn't see them, but when their dogs started whimpering and scratching at the walls for no apparent reason, they would say, "Bowser must have smelled a rat."

THAT'S HOGWASH.

Meaning: That's nonsense.

Story: Hogwash was a limp watery substance that was fed to pigs. It contained leftover scraps and some flour, but nothing very substantial.

ANOTHER MAD COW

Boolah, boolah! Where's your moolah?

DIAMOND IN THE ROUGH

In 2004 a diamond merchant in India hid a bag full of
1,700 small diamonds in a pile of hay at his home.
Unfortunately, his cow ate the hay…and the bag. Since
cows are sacred in India, it never occurred to him to kill
the cow to get the bag. Instead, he followed the cow
around everywhere, picking one diamond at a time out
of the cow's poop.

ANIMAL NEWS

CAT WINS BIG!

One winter's night in 1996 a man named Gayle McManamon saw his cat, Skipper, playing with his lottery shaker (a simple device that some people use to help them pick their lottery numbers). He noticed that Skipper had picked six numbers: 8, 11, 16, 25, 26, and 42.

So the very next day McManamon bought a lottery ticket with the cat's numbers. And amazingly—you guessed it—he won. How much? $3.72 million!

BOOK HOUND

Read all about it.

Wofford, a golden retriever from Norfolk, Virginia, likes to fetch, all right—but not sticks or balls. Wofford is a book hound. He *loves* books. Even as a young pup, Wofford liked to take books to bed with him. He often greets guests at the door by offering them a book. One day Wofford got out of the yard and slipped into the public library. He picked up a children's book and waited in line to check it out. The librarian took the book and tried to offer Wofford a chew toy instead, but Wofford would have none of it. He headed right back to the stacks and got himself another book.

SPIRIT GUIDES

Many cultures believe that an animal's spirit enters into a person when they are born. Which animal are you?

CAT

Serene

You are extremely independent—no one can tell you what to do. But you can be lovable and playful when you want to be. Above all you are serene, graceful, and love to relax.

BEAR

Patient

You are a patient and wise friend. You love your family but you are just as happy being alone. You may enjoy fishing, hiking, and wrestling with your friends.

DOG

Loyal

You are a loving, fun, and loyal pal. You are eager to help and are always the first to volunteer. You are protective—you can smell trouble coming from a mile away.

DOLPHIN
Cheerful

You are friendly, outgoing, and trustworthy. You know how to find the balance between work and play. You love to talk and you might even like to write or sing.

EAGLE
Alert

You are courageous, observant, and thoughtful. If you are missing, all anyone needs to do is look up—you're probably in a tree watching the world.

ELEPHANT
Compassionate

You are strong and compassionate. You see every moment as an opportunity to learn and you never forget. You love being with your family and friends.

GIRAFFE
Aware

You are intuitive and can see far into the future. You aren't afraid to take risks because you are able to see your dreams come true.

HIPPOPOTAMUS

Protective

You are a gentle soul. Yet when it comes to your home and family you are fiercely protective. You are very inventive and know how to have a good time.

HORSE

Faithful

You are a faithful and wise friend. You find creative solutions to life's problems. You love to travel—especially with a group.

LION

Proud

You are the center of attention—you can't help it. You love playing, working, or just hanging with your family and friends. You know how to chill.

MONKEY

Imaginative

You are energetic, imaginative, and creative. You have a knack for inventing and love to play practical jokes on your family and friends.

PIG
Honorable
You are truthful and honorable—you look out for the little guy. You are smart enough to know that the simple pleasures in life are the best.

RABBIT
Creative
You are creative and intelligent. Being quick thinking, you are an excellent problem solver. You enjoy life— "No Fear" is your motto.

SNAKE
Charming
You are a creative and ambitious leader. Charm is your middle name. Your friends think you are mysterious because you love illusions and have a talent for magic.

TIGER
Powerful
Energetic and powerful, you know what you want and you get it. You are also mischievous and love a good surprise.

VIP'S VIPS
(VERY IMPORTANT PEOPLE'S VERY IMPORTANT PETS)

President Teddy Roosevelt's family had quite a menagerie, including a lion, a hyena, a coyote, five bears, a badger, two parrots, a zebra, a raccoon, an owl, cats, dogs, horses, guinea pigs, and a snake named Emily Spinach. Their pet pony, Algonquin, made a number of secret trips up the White House elevator to visit young Archibald Roosevelt when he was ill.

Lord Byron, the poet, was not allowed to keep a dog in his rooms at Cambridge University in England. So he kept a pet bear instead.

Walt Disney owned a pet mouse named Mortimer, which was the inspiration for the famous cartoon mouse. His wife Lillian didn't like the name, so he changed it to Mickey Mouse.

MEET PORKCHOP

The Keekorok Lodge in Kenya has an unusual "guard dog" who gallops out to greet the guests. She's a warthog named Porkchop. Porkchop was only two weeks old when she was found stuck in some bushes in the Masai Mara Game Reserve. The lodge owners adopted her and now this little warthog trots around the grounds, pays visits to sunbathers by the pool, and is even up for a game of fetch. However, one roar from hippos in the nearby pond and Porkchop's tail stands straight up and she runs for the nearest place to hide, which could be behind your legs or in your lap!

SNORKEL MASTERS

Did you know that elephants can snorkel? They can walk along the bottom of a river with just the tip of their trunks sticking out for air. They have even been seen snorkeling far out at sea. Some scientists think elephants may have evolved from water creatures because of their snorkeling ability.

DID YOU KNOW?

• Elephants' eyes are only slightly larger than humans'.

• The average elephant weighs less than a blue whale's tongue.

• There are 40,000 muscles in an elephant's trunk.

• Elephants can hear the footsteps of a mouse.

• Elephants cry when a loved one dies.

THEY NEVER FORGET

CASE #1. When a female elephant named Kura was brought to the Shambala Preserve in California, the keepers worried that she wouldn't get along with Timbo, a bull elephant who already lived there. But the moment they saw each other, the two elephants wrapped their trunks together like old friends. It turned out that they had been shipped from Africa on the same freighter more than 40 years earlier.

CASE #2. An elephant in a game park in Kenya had a badly injured foot but wouldn't let anyone get near him to treat it. Finally the vets sent for the elephant's old trainer. He hadn't seen the elephant for 15 years, but the minute he called the elephant by name, it lay down and held up the hurt foot so the vets could take care of it.

THE ELEPHANT AND THE COWBOY

ORPHAN AMY MEETS BOB

When Amy the elephant first met Bob the cowboy, she was just a baby. She was also an orphan—one of five that had been brought to the United States from Africa by a man who rented stalls at Bob's T-Cross Ranch in Pueblo, Colorado. The man's plan was to sell the orphaned elephants to zoos or circuses. But Amy was sickly and undersized and nobody wanted her...except Bob.

RANCH HAND

Bob Norris saw something special in the tiny elephant,

and he decided to adopt her. The T-Cross Ranch was a working ranch, so Bob put Amy to work, too. He taught her how to lead a horse, separate a single cow from the herd, and feed the goats. When she wasn't working, he taught Amy how to play the piano and the harmonica. She also played with giant beach balls and stuffed animals. Bob took her to the local schools to teach children about elephants. Amy even had her favorite restaurants. She'd wait patiently in the back of the truck while Bob would run in to El Chorros and get her favorite food: sticky buns.

AMY JOINS THE CIRCUS

By the time she was seven, Amy had become too big to live on the ranch. So Bob got her a job with the Big Apple Circus. Amy loved the circus and the circus loved her. But Bob missed Amy more than he'd ever imagined he would. A year later Bob and his wife flew to New York to see Amy perform. They sat in the front row. Bob had brought Amy's

favorite sticky buns from El Chorros. He was very nervous: would Amy even know who he was anymore?

AMY AND BOB, TOGETHER AGAIN

The lights came on and the clowns and performers ran
into the ring. Finally came the star of the show: Amy.
She began her act—and suddenly stopped. Her trunk
went up and she sniffed the air. She rumbled and trum-
peted. The crowd froze.

What was Amy doing? Suddenly she ran straight to
Bob, dropped to her knees, and laid her head in his lap.
She touched the tip of her trunk under his chin and all
over his face. She made the chirruping sound she always
made when she was happy. Bob wrapped his arms around
Amy and cried, "She remembers me!"

HOMEWARD BOUND

In his book The Parrot's Lament, *author Eugene Linden tells the story of a remarkable leopard named Harriet.*

As a cub, Harriet had been rescued and taken into the home of a conservationist named Billy Arjun Singh. He raised Harriet to adulthood, then returned her to the forest preserve across the river in northern India where she was born. Harriet's return to the wild was successful and she soon gave birth to two cubs of her own. Everything was fine until the flood season came. As the water rose and filled her den, Harriet quickly had to find a safe place for her cubs.

Where'd she go? Home. One by one, she carried her cubs across the rising river to Billy Singh's house. The leopards stayed in Singh's kitchen until the floodwaters receded. Then she was ready to return to the preserve. She tried to carry the cubs across the river, but the current was too strong. Thinking quickly, Harriet took the cubs to Singh's boat, where she had ridden many times, and dropped her children inside. Then she climbed into the boat and patiently waited until Singh ferried her and her family safely across the raging river, back to her den.

"These amazing true stories confirm what many of us have always suspected — that animals would make better humans than most humans would."
—CARL HIAASEN

THE
Parrot's LAMENT

AND OTHER TRUE TALES OF
ANIMAL INTRIGUE,
INTELLIGENCE, AND INGENUITY

EUGENE LINDEN

YO DUDE!

How do animals say hello?

HIPPOS are the only animals that can communicate above *and* below the water.

KANGAROO RATS talk by stamping their feet.

PRAIRIE DOGS have one of the most sophisticated animal languages known to science, with more than 100 "words."

GIRAFFES press their necks together when they're courting.

EXPOSED!

Hold on to your pants. It's a jungle out there!

Raja was a 14-year-old orangutan who lived at an ape sanctuary on the Pacific island of Borneo. One day Raja surprised a French tourist by grabbing him, stripping off his shirt, pants, and underwear, and then running off into the forest. The startled Frenchman was left standing alone on the trail…naked.

YIKES, STRIPES!

*What's black and white and runs all over…Africa?
Answer: the zebra—one of Africa's strangest
creatures. Zebras live in the savannas of
central Africa, and they're closely
related to the horse.*

It's official: Zebras are white with black stripes, not
the other way around. So why are they striped?
Experts say it's to confuse predators—from lions to tiny
tsetse flies—who can't tell where one zebra begins and
the other ends. Zebras are instinctively attracted to
anything with black-and-white stripes. Even if the
stripes are painted on a wall, a zebra will go stand next
to them!

Although zebras can be ridden, they can never be domesticated like horses can. Humans have tried for 200 years to get zebras to act like horses, but the zebras refuse to cooperate—they are just too wild and unpredictable to be trained.

DID YOU KNOW?

• No two zebra stripe patterns are alike.

• A zebra crossed with a horse is a *zorse*. A zebra crossed with a donkey is a *zonkey*.

• A zebra's night vision is as good as an owl's.

• Zebras smile. They greet each other with a bared-teeth grimace that helps prevent aggression.

• Zebras travel in herds of as many as 10,000.

• Although most zebras are white with black stripes, a few are actually black with white stripes.

WHAT A BABY!

BABY HARP SEALS are born with totally white fur. The fur provides camouflage on snow and ice. It changes to waterproof, dark brown fur as they grow older.

NEWBORN DUCK-BILLED PLATYPUSES have teeth that help them break out of their eggs. The teeth disappear as they get older.

NEWBORN ARMADILLOS have soft shells, like human fingernails. A natural process called *ossification* causes their shells to harden into bone.

BAT BABIES have no hair when they're born. To keep the babies warm, all of the mother bats and babies huddle together in a bat nursery.

NEWBORN SKUNKS are born hairless with striped black-and-white skin. Their eyes and ears are closed, but careful—they can still spray!

BABY BUFFALO are born without horns or a hump—they start to form when the baby is two months old.

NEWBORN BUSH BABIES are just two inches long and weigh only ½ ounce (about the weight of a tablespoon of water). Bush babies can grow up to be eight inches long—but they will always sound like crybabies. (That's why they're called bush *babies*.)

POLAR PLUS

WALRUSES use their tusks like canes to walk on land.

The male walrus with the longest tusks usually becomes the leader.

Walruses don't hunt for food with their tusks, but they do use their whiskers, which can sense the movement of fish.

CARIBOU can sleep in water.

SEALS can hold their breath for more than an hour and dive down nearly a mile in the ocean.

Ever seen a seal scoot across the ground? That scooting motion is known as *galluphing*.

AN ARCTIC FOX'S fur can keep it warm and toasty at 100 degrees below zero. At that temperature, you would freeze to death in less than five minutes.

Arctic fox dens are used for centuries, by many generations of foxes. Over the years they become so big that they can have more than 100 entrances.

WOLF TALK

According to scientists, wolves have a unique way of communicating. Here's how it works.

BARK: Warning! Danger!

BARED TEETH: Don't come any closer.

WHIMPER: Mother does this to calm the pups.

HEAD AND EARS UP HIGH: I'm the boss.

EARS BACK AND SQUINT: I'm afraid.

DANCE AND BOW: Want to play?

HIGH WHINE OR SQUEAKING SOUND: Puppies come here!

WAG JUST THE TIP OF THE TAIL: I'm about to attack.

TAIL BETWEEN LEGS: You're the boss.

WOLF HOWL: Everyone! Bring the pack together!

DID YOU KNOW?

- A wolf's pawprint can be bigger than a human hand.
- A wolf's tail hangs, while a dog's tail tends to stick up.
- Every wolf pack has a leader. He's called the alpha male.

GOING BATTY

- There are about 1,000 types of bats.

- Disc-winged bats of South America have sticky patches on their wings and feet, which allow them to live inside banana leaves.

- Bats are the only mammals that can truly fly.

- Generally, bats will turn left when coming out of a cave.

- The scientific name for bat is *Chiroptera*, which is Greek for "hand-wing."

- Vampire bats adopt orphans.

- A bat's leg bones are too thin to walk on.

- Woolly bats of West Africa live in the large webs of colonial spiders.

- A bat can eat as many as 1,200 insects in an hour.

- Texas has more bats than any other state. Bracken Cave alone is home to 20 million Mexican free-tailed bats.

LIFE ON EASY CREEK

In 2004 someone pulled a heist at the Lucky Dollar Casino in Greensburg, Louisiana, and stole $75,000. Sheriff's deputies tracked down the crooks but couldn't find the stolen money. Then a lawyer hoping to make a deal for one of the crooks called prosecutors and revealed that the money had been tossed into a nearby creek.

Officers raced to the creek and found one of the money bags floating in the brush and another leaning against a beaver dam.

When they drained the pond, they found the third bag…empty. Apparently a pair of beavers had found it first, and had woven thousands of soggy bills into the walls of their dam. When cops broke open the dam to retrieve the bills, they couldn't believe their eyes—the interior looked like it had been decorated with money wallpaper!

WRONG!

Some animal names just don't fit.

FLYING FOXES aren't foxes. They're bats. They live in Australia and they're huge. In fact, with a wingspan of up to six feet, they're the largest bats in the world! And, unlike foxes, they eat only fruit.

MOUNTAIN BEAVERS aren't beavers and they don't live in the mountains. They are muskratlike rodents that live mostly in the coastal forests of the Pacific Northwest. With their short stubby bodies and no tail, they look like groundhogs.

CRABEATER SEALS do *not* eat crabs! They eat krill, a tiny shrimplike animal in the icy waters around Antarctica. They were misnamed in 1837 by the French explorer Jules Dumont d'Urville.

PRAIRIE DOGS are not dogs—they're rodents. They live in large underground colonies called townships. However, they do have a sharp bark that sounds like a dog's.

PICK THE WEIRDEST NOSE

STAR-NOSED MOLES

have the most complex noses in the animal kingdom. Their noses have tentacles, which they use to detect insect prey. No other nose is as sensitive to the touch (or as weird looking) as the star-nosed mole's.

BATS can detect the warmth of an animal from six inches away using their "nose-leaf."

The male **PROBOSCIS MONKEY** has a really big nose—sometimes it's so big the monkey has to hold it aside with one hand to eat! The purpose of the giant schnoz is unclear, but scientists think it may help the monkeys stay cool in the humid swamps of southeast Asia.

ANIMAL NEWS
INVASION OF THE ARMADILLOS

A stranger is taking over our farms, forests, and neighborhoods! An invader from Central America, protected by bands of sturdy

body armor, is expanding its range across the United States 10 times faster than other mammals. As many as 50 million of these invaders are already here.

Who is this creature? It's the nine-banded armadillo. This rabbit-sized mammal prospers in areas where others fail. Why? Because the armadillo not only has lots of babies but also chooses when to have them. The pregnant female can delay birth for up to two years until she finds a safe place to raise her kids. (The armadillo is the only mammal that always has four identical girls or boys.) Plus, an armadillo can live up to 20 years, which means that just a few armadillos can quickly take over a new area.

Can anything stop the armadillo from overrunning North America? Yes. Cold. Armadillos don't like it. They can't survive temperatures below freezing. So those of you in Alaska, Montana, Minnesota, and all of those icy northern states can relax. The armadillo invasion won't be coming your way.

ARMOR-DILLOS

• There are 20 species of armadillo, but the nine-banded armadillo is the only one that lives in North America. The other 19 live in South America.

• Startle an armadillo and it will jump three to four feet straight up in the air!

• Armadillos walk on their tiptoes.

• The giant armadillo can weigh over 120 pounds and be up to five feet long.

• Armadillos eat six *billion* pounds of bugs in the U.S. every year!

• An armadillo without its shell looks like a hairless rabbit.

WILD AND WOOLLY FACT

Armadillos are the submarines of the animal world. Their heavy shells make them sink, so they can walk along the bottom of a river. If they want to float, they gulp air into their intestines and float on the surface like a balloon.

BRIGHT IDEAS

Some examples of how humans take care of troubled animals.

PROBLEM: Too many squirrels from a rare colony in England were being killed while crossing a busy highway.

SOLUTION: The authorities built rope bridges to help the squirrels get safely to the other side of the road.

PROBLEM: Orphaned baby kangaroos, or *joeys*, can't survive for long outside their mother's pouch.

SOLUTION: Australians make cotton "joey bags" that resemble kangaroo pouches and hang them from baby bouncer frames. The orphan joey stays inside until it grows fur and can survive on its own.

PROBLEM: During a fire, pets are far more sensitive to the effects of smoke than humans are.

SOLUTION: A Florida fire department got some specially sized oxygen masks from a local vet. Now cats, dogs, and even hamsters suffering from smoke inhalation can be given a breath of life-saving air.

LIONS AND TIGERS AND BEARS, OH MY!

Chantek is an orangutan who was taught sign language by Dr. H. Lyn Miles and lived on the University of Tennessee campus. When the Ringling Brothers and Barnum & Bailey Circus came to town, he was invited to meet the other animals. All went well

until the orangutan was offered a chance to pet a tiger. Chantek was so scared he jumped out of Miles's arms and ran all the way across the university campus, across the football field, and back into his trailer.

Still not feeling safe, he flipped over a sign that said he and Miles were out but would return soon, then locked two sets of doors, climbed into his hammock...and pulled the covers over his head.

GHOST PETS

GHOST RIDERS IN THE SKY

In the suburbs of Chicago there is a horseriding trail that crosses a very busy street. Over its long history, many riders and horses have been killed trying to cross the street. A traffic light was finally placed there, which made it much safer. But now, when it's night or near dusk, some drivers have reported seeing what appears to be a horse and rider trying to cross the street. The motorists slow down, trying to get a better view, and suddenly the ghostly duo just disappears into thin air. Other ghostly steeds have been seen: one throwing his rider from the saddle and another being dragged sideways down the highway.

WAKE UP, WALTER!

One day, Walter Manuel of Los Angeles dreamed that his dog Lady was barking frantically trying to wake him. Lady had died just three weeks earlier, but the dream seemed so real that he couldn't help rushing to the bedroom window to see if anything was wrong. He was shocked to see his two-year-old son fall into the swimming pool. Thanks to Lady's ghost, Manuel was able to save his little boy.

WATER DOGS

They're wet and wild (and woolly).

SCUBA-DOO

Shadow is a half golden, half Labrador retriever from Boynton Beach, Florida, who loves to spend time not just *in* the water—but *under* the water. Shadow is a scuba diver. Using special dive gear designed by her owner, Dwane Folsom, Shadow can stay underwater for an hour. Her favorite dive buddy, other than Dwane, is a moray eel.

X-TREME MASTER

Part-X is running out of extreme sports to try. This Jack Russell terrier from Cornwall, England, has mastered surfing, cliff-jumping, rappelling, and sea kayaking. Now he's learning to water ski in his own custom-made life jacket. Part-X got the bug for extreme sports in 2000 when he jumped on his owner's surf board and rode his first wave. "Whenever we go near moving water Part-X gets really, really excited," says owner J.P. Eatock. "He even tries to woof and bite the wave as we surf." Next: crossing the Irish Sea by kayak and a tandem sky dive with J.P.

I'M BACK!

Three stories about pets that found their way home.

AUSTRALIAN WALKABOUT. In October 1973 a collie named Whisky became separated from his master while vacationing in Darwin in northern Australia. Nine months later, Whisky had found his way home. The collie had traveled an amazing 1,802 miles across Australia—and through the rugged Outback—to reach the southern city of Melbourne...and his master's home.

DODGING BULLETS. When Private James Brown went to France to fight in World War I, he left his Irish terrier, Prince, at home in England. A month later, on September 27, 1914, his wife wrote to him with the sad news that Prince was missing. The letter didn't upset Private Brown—his devoted dog had already joined him in the trenches. Prince had somehow crossed the English Channel (probably as a stowaway on a boat) and walked another 60 miles through battlefields to find his best friend in Armentières, France. That was a trip of 200 miles.

MARATHON CAT. A tabby cat named McCavity didn't like his new home in Cumbernauld, Scotland, even though his family was with him. One day he just up and left. Three weeks and 497 miles later, McCavity was found meowing at the front door of his old home in Truro, England. McCavity had walked 25 miles a day for 21 days—that's almost a marathon a day.

DREAMING OF CATS

According to some dream experts...

- If you dream of a **tortoise-shell cat**, you'll be **lucky in love**.

- If you dream of a **ginger (orange) cat**, you'll be **lucky in money and business**.

- If you dream of a **tabby cat**, you'll be **lucky at home**.

- If you dream of a **black-and-white cat**, you'll be **lucky with children**.

- If you dream of a **multi-colored cat**, you'll be **lucky with making new friends**.

- If you dream of a **black cat**, you'll be **lucky in all things**.

FOND FAREWELLS

They loved their pets so much that when they died...

King Charles IX of France had his greyhound Courte made into hunting gloves.

King Edward VII of England had his terrier Jack's hair made into a bracelet.

Roy Rogers, the singing cowboy movie star of the 1950s, had his horse, Trigger, and his dog, Bullet, stuffed and put on display at the Roy Rogers and Dale Evans Museum in Branson, Missouri.

∪ ∪ ∪

ANIMAL EPITAPHS

A few funny epitaphs found on tombstones in New York's Hartsdale Canine Cemetery, America's first pet cemetery.

Grumpy
"His sympathetic love and understanding enriched our lives"

Penny
"She never knew she was a rabbit"

Thor Dog
"A cat"

Hoppy
"Our three-legged wonder"

GOTTA GO!

PACHYDERM POTTY

Elephants in Thailand are already taught to paint, dance, and play musical instruments. What's next? They're being toilet trained.

PHOTO CREDITS

Uncle John's Bathroom Readers For Kids Only!

Uncle John's Bathroom Reader
For Kids Only!
© 2002. $12.95
288 pages, illustrated.

Uncle John's **Electrifying**
Bathroom Reader For Kids Only!
© 2003. $12.95
288 pages, illustrated.

Uncle John's **Top Secret!**
Bathroom Reader For Kids Only!
© 2004. $12.95
288 pages, illustrated.

Uncle John's **Book of Fun**
© 2004. $12.95
288 pages, illustrated.

To order, contact:
Bathroom Readers' Press
P.O. Box 1117, Ashland, OR 97520
Phone: 888-488-4642 Fax: 541-482-6159
www.bathroomreader.com

THE LAST PAGE

FELLOW BATHROOM READERS
Bathroom reading should never be taken
loosely, so Sit Down and Be Counted!
Join the Bathroom Readers' Institute. It's free!
Just go to *www.bathroomreader.com* to sign
up. Or send a self-addressed, stamped
envelope and your email address to:
Bathroom Readers' Institute, P.O. Box 1117,
Ashland, Oregon 97520. You'll receive a free member-
ship card, our BRI newsletter (sent out via e-mail),
discounts when ordering directly through the BRI, and
you'll earn a permanent spot on the BRI honor roll!

UNCLE JOHN'S NEXT
BATHROOM READER FOR KIDS ONLY
IS ALREADY IN THE WORKS!

Is there a subject you'd like to read about
in our next *Uncle John's Bathroom Reader* for
kids? Write to us at *www.bathroomreader.com*
and let us know. We aim to please.

Well, we're out of space, and when
you've got to go, you've got to go. Hope
to hear from you soon. Meanwhile,
remember...

Go with the Flow!